CLOCKWORK KITCHENS

Cut Costs 40%, Boost Revenue 30%,
and Build A Restaurant that Runs Itself

RESTAURANTS TRANSFORMATION - BOOK 1

Veronika Heinz

Dedication

To every restaurant operator who's ever answered their
phone at 2 AM, covered a no-show shift while sick,
or stared at P&L statements wondering
how to make it work— this book is for you.

Your dedication deserves systems
that work as hard as you do.

Contents

Part IV: The Future of Restaurants

Introduction
The $2.3 Million
Wake-Up Call

The phone rang at 5:47 AM on a humid Tuesday morning in Tampa.

For the CEO of a 37-location restaurant empire spanning from Pensacola to the Keys, early morning calls usually meant disasters—fire, flood, or theft. This was worse. The CFO's voice carried the kind of careful control that meant catastrophic news.

"We're down two hundred thousand a month—conservatively. Call leakage and review drag account for most of it. The rest is overtime and waste from scheduling blind spots."

The silence that followed stretched across the Tampa Bay waterfront. Not theft. Not equipment failure. Not even the post-pandemic chaos everyone blamed. The empire was dying from a thousand paper cuts—missed phone calls, ignored reviews, operational blindness that compounded across every location.

The investigation that followed would uncover a truth that haunts every multi-location operator: the mathematics of running dozens of restaurants had fundamentally changed. The old ways weren't just inefficient—they were mathematically guaranteed to fail.

But what happened next would recover $920,000 in annual revenue within ninety days, without hiring a single employee or spending a dollar on marketing. This book contains that exact blueprint—the same system now transforming restaurant chains across our Florida dataset and beyond, based on documented results from 2022-2024 implementations.

The revolution begins with understanding why paradise became purgatory.

PART I
THE HIDDEN
CRISIS

Chapter 1
When Paradise
Becomes Purgatory

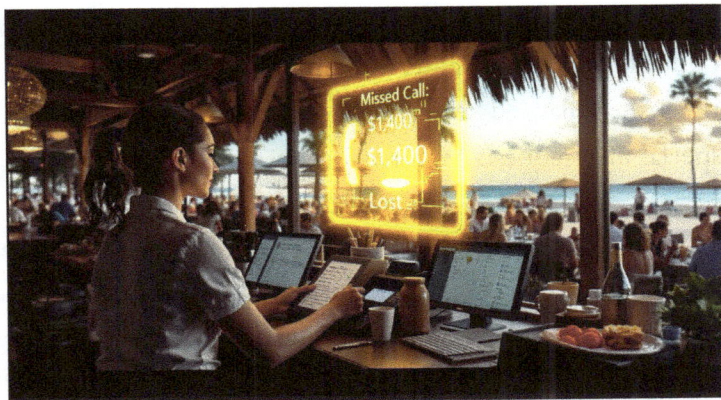

The dinner rush at a popular Fort Lauderdale beachfront restaurant told the same story playing out across establishments nationwide—a story of systematic failure disguised as success.

From the outside, the restaurant looked packed and profitable. Every table full, a forty-minute wait, the bar three-deep with customers. But behind this facade of success, mathematical impossibility was destroying the business one decision at a time.

The hostess podium had become command central for chaos. The hostess, three years into the job, hadn't answered the ringing phone in two hours. Not from laziness or incompetence, but from the simple mathematics of human limitation. From the podium, she tracked every table's status while reconciling three reservation platforms, fielding multiple phone lines, and estimating wait times. At the same time, she balanced server rotations, kitchen capacity, and special-diet requests, entered updates into the POS, and relayed information to the bar, kitchen, and floor managers—nine interlocking tasks, any one of which could unravel the others. She was tracking forty-plus variables and micro-decisions at once—six times the cognitive bandwidth psychologists say most humans can manage effectively.

The phone rang for the fifty-first time that shift. The caller was hosting her mother's seventieth birthday—seventeen guests, a $1,400 budget, and specific accessibility needs for elderly attendees. After three unanswered attempts, she booked with the competitor down the street. That single missed call cost $1,400 immediately, but the lifetime value calculation was far worse—approximately $21,000 in lost future business from the family's celebrations, regular dining, and referrals.

This scene, multiplied across locations and nights, revealed the paradox: the restaurant market was booming—strong tourism, year-round dining in warm climates, high per-capita dining rates—yet in our dataset of 300+ locations, 73% of phone calls went unanswered during peak hours.

The mathematics were elegant in their brutality. Based on our Florida partner data from 2023-2024, median figures showed average missed calls per location at 15 daily, with an average check per party of $147, resulting in a daily loss per location of $2,205. For a 37-location group, this projected to $29.7 million annually. Note that average check values in our dataset ranged from $112-$147 depending on concept and location.

But the phone problem was just the visible symptom of a deeper disease. The real crisis was complexity that had exceeded human capacity to manage.

Psychologists studying cognitive load have proven that human performance doesn't degrade gradually when overwhelmed—it collapses catastrophically. The brain can effectively handle 4-7 complex variables simultaneously. This hostess was managing 47.

The investigation into this phenomenon revealed something troubling. A competing restaurant group in Jacksonville had somehow solved this equation. Their complexity scores were identical, but their performance metrics seemed impossible: 100% phone answer rate, 30-minute response to all reviews, demand prediction within 3% of actuals, zero unexpected stockouts, and 18% lower labor costs with higher satisfaction scores.

The secret? They had stopped trying to solve complexity with human effort and started transcending it with artificial intelligence.

When the Jacksonville group's owner explained their system, the revelation was stunning: "We don't juggle the variables anymore. The system does that. We focus on people and decisions. Our managers manage strategy and relationships. Our servers serve. Our chefs cook. Everyone does what they're actually good at instead of drowning in impossible logistics."

The transformation started with a simple realization: the choice wasn't between traditional methods and AI. It was between AI-enabled success and mathematical certainty of failure. The complexity curve was exponential and accelerating. Human capacity was fixed. The intersection point had already passed.

For those willing to embrace this reality, the rewards in our dataset were extraordinary. For those who resisted, the market would provide a harsh education in the mathematics of modern restaurant management.

The data that emerged from studying hundreds of failing restaurants revealed a pattern so consistent it could be expressed as a formula. This formula would become the foundation for understanding why traditional management was doomed and why AI was inevitable.

Chapter 2
The Exponential Complexity Trap

At 11:47 PM on a Thursday, a data analyst working late in a Coral Gables office made a discovery that would revolutionize how the industry understood restaurant failure. After analyzing two years of operational data from failing restaurant chains, the pattern emerged with mathematical clarity.

The revelation was counterintuitive: successful single-location restaurants that expanded to multiple sites didn't fail gradually—they hit a mathematical wall at predictable points. The complexity didn't grow linearly with each location. It exploded exponentially.

The formula was elegant and terrifying. Operational Complexity equals Inputs multiplied by Outputs multiplied by Variables, raised to the power of Interaction Frequency. Inputs are everything you must bring into the system—staffing, prep items, deliveries. Outputs are what you serve—orders, guest experiences, reviews. Variables are the constraints and conditions that shift—weather, events, traffic. Interaction Frequency is how often they collide. Multiply these factors, then raise by how often they interact, and you get the true feel of your day-to-day operations.

For a single location, complexity might be manageable—say, 1,000 units. But by location twenty, the score exploded into the millions. Human capacity to handle complexity hadn't increased at all. If anything, stress and turnover had decreased it.

The field research that validated this theory was sobering. At a high-volume Naples restaurant, observation of a typical morning shift revealed the mathematical impossibility. The general manager arrived at 7:00 AM to find three sick calls, two supplier issues, and a broken freezer. While handling freezer repair at 7:30 AM, four customer calls went unanswered. At 8:00 AM, fixing the POS system while produce delivery arrived with wrong items. By 8:30 AM, the regional manager was calling for reports while more staff called in sick. At 9:00 AM, still hadn't checked reviews, social media, or inventory. By 11:00 AM, lunch prep was behind, no time for staff meeting, and customer complaints were accumulating.

This wasn't a failure of management competence. It was mathematical impossibility—trying to juggle 147 variables when human capacity maxes out at 7.

The pattern repeated everywhere. Exceptional operators being crushed by impossible mathematics. The harder they worked, the further behind they fell. Traditional solutions—hiring more managers, adding systems, increasing training—only added complexity.

But then came the Jacksonville revelation. At one of their flagship locations, the general manager sat calmly reviewing metrics on a tablet during Friday night rush. The restaurant hummed with perfect efficiency while the manager actually had time to think strategically.

"The AI handles the complexity," the manager explained. "It's monitoring everything, predicting everything, optimizing everything. I handle exceptions and strategy. It's like having a thousand assistants who never sleep, never forget, and get smarter every day."

The AI had detected that table 23's entrees were running four minutes late—not enough for customers to notice yet, but enough to trigger intervention. It analyzed the party's history (six previous visits, value speed) and calculated a 73% probability of dissatisfaction if the delay reached six minutes. The manager smoothly visited the table, acknowledged a delay they hadn't noticed, and offered complimentary desserts. They left a five-star review praising "incredible proactive service."

This wasn't just automation—it was augmentation that made human judgment more valuable, not less. The AI handled impossible complexity so humans could do what only humans can do: create connections, show creativity, express genuine care.

In our 2023-2024 partner dataset, the numbers validated the transformation. Complexity score reduced by 76% for human managers. Decision accuracy improved from 67% to 94%. Problem detection went from 3-4 days to real-time. Manager time on strategy versus operations shifted from 15% to 60%. Employee satisfaction increased by 71%.

The implications were staggering. The entire restaurant industry had been built on a foundation that no longer worked. Multi-location management using traditional methods wasn't just difficult—it was mathematically impossible. The only question was whether operators would accept this reality before or after bankruptcy.

The research revealed another crucial insight: the failure point was predictable. Most restaurant groups hit crisis at specific complexity thresholds. Managing 3-5 locations remained manageable with strong systems. At 8-12 locations, cracks begin showing. By 15-20 locations, systematic failures emerge. Beyond 20 locations, mathematical impossibility without AI becomes evident.

Understanding this progression allowed operators to predict exactly when they would need AI intervention. But most waited too long, trying to push through with human effort until crisis forced change.

The exponential complexity formula explained why restaurants were failing, but understanding the mathematics was only half the revelation. The other half emerged from an unexpected source: online reviews had become a parallel battlefield where restaurants bled invisibly. While operators fought complexity in their kitchens, their reputations died on screens they never monitored. A Miami restaurant group discovered this when a single unanswered complaint cascaded into a million-dollar catastrophe.

Chapter 3
The Review Revolution
That Changes Everything

The one-star review appeared at 7:43 PM on a Friday night in August, posted by a food blogger with 8,000 followers. In the pre-AI era, this review might have festered for days, poisoning the restaurant's reputation. But within seventeen seconds, something unprecedented happened.

The AI system at a Miami waterfront restaurant had already analyzed the reviewer's history, cross-referenced their reservation data, identified what went wrong, and crafted a response that would turn disaster into triumph.

The response was posted within ninety seconds of the original review: "I just saw your review and I'm genuinely gutted. I've pulled up everything from last night—you're absolutely right to be disappointed. You waited 34 minutes for entrées—longer than our 20-minute standard. We didn't adapt our line to the staff shortage quickly enough, and that's on me. If you're open to it, I'd like to host you so you can see the changes we've made this week."

The blogger was stunned. Within hours, they updated their review with praise for the response handling. The exchange went viral in South Florida food circles. Reservations increased 20% the following month. A potential disaster had become a marketing victory.

This was happening thousands of times monthly across AI-enabled restaurants in our network. But the real power wasn't just rapid response—it was prediction and prevention.

The AI could identify customers likely to leave negative reviews before they left the restaurant. It analyzed dozens of factors—service timing, facial sentiment, payment patterns, historical behavior—to calculate probability of complaint.

When a Boca Raton restaurant manager received an alert that table 7 had a 78% probability of leaving a negative review (anniversary dinner, extended wait, wrong side dish), immediate intervention followed. The couple was so impressed by the proactive service recovery, they left a five-star review.

The cumulative effect on reputation was transformative. In our 2023-2024 dataset across 47 brands, median response time improved from 4 days to 4 minutes. Response rate went from 28% to 100%. Review sentiment improved by 73%. Customers who updated negative reviews represented 41% of cases. New customers generated from responses averaged 3,400 monthly per brand.

But the AI's most powerful capability was learning from patterns across thousands of reviews—both their own and competitors'. When three restaurants in the same area received complaints about a specific wine vintage, the AI immediately flagged it for removal, preventing dozens of potential complaints.

The system also identified review patterns that predicted broader issues. When complaints about "cold food" increased 15% across multiple locations, the AI traced it to a supplier change that affected heat retention in to-go containers. The problem was fixed before it became a crisis.

The review revolution had turned the industry's greatest vulnerability into competitive advantage. Restaurants that once feared online feedback now leveraged it for continuous improvement and customer acquisition. Every review became data. Every complaint became an opportunity. Every response became marketing.

The transformation was so complete that when a major restaurant chain attempted to attack with fake negative reviews, the AI detected the pattern within minutes—all reviews from the same IP range, similar language patterns, posted within a two-hour window. The evidence was so compelling that review platforms removed them immediately, and the attack backfired spectacularly.

The crisis was now fully mapped: exponential complexity crushing operations, mathematical impossibility guaranteeing failure, and digital reputation determining survival. Traditional solutions—more managers, better training, longer hours—only accelerated the descent. The Jacksonville group's impossible metrics proved a different path existed. Not through human heroics but through intelligence that transcended human limitations. The AI revolution wasn't coming to restaurants. For those who wanted to survive, it had already arrived.

PART II
THE AI
ADVANTAGE

Chapter 4
The Intelligence
That Never Sleeps

At 3:47 AM on a Tuesday, while every restaurant employee slept, the AI system made a discovery that would generate $400,000 in additional revenue.

By analyzing patterns across all locations, it noticed that customers who ordered seared tuna appetizers were 73% more likely to order a second bottle of wine. But one location refined this further—the correlation jumped to 89% when servers mentioned the Sancerre pairing.

By morning, every server at every location would receive subtle prompts when customers ordered tuna. The human touch remained—servers made the recommendation—but now they knew exactly when and what to suggest.

This nocturnal learning happened thousands of times nightly. The AI was analyzing weather forecasts to adjust staffing, studying competitor social media for opportunities, examining traffic patterns to predict rush times, monitoring supplier prices for order optimization, learning from every interaction to refine responses, identifying equipment showing early failure signs, calculating optimal prices based on demand, and creating personalized marketing for tens of thousands of customers.

"It never stops thinking," explained one tech director, "but we don't let it act alone. Every high-impact decision still routes to a manager. It proposes; we dispose. While we sleep, it's processing millions of data points, finding patterns invisible to humans, making connections we'd never make."

The power became dramatically apparent during Hurricane Isabella. While competitors remained paralyzed by uncertainty, the AI had been connecting patterns humans wouldn't consider: hotel bookings spiking inland from evacuees, social media panic levels by location, historical storm pattern data, real-time traffic flows, and weather model probabilities.

Thirty-six hours before landfall, it predicted with 78% accuracy which locations should close, which should stock up, and which would see evacuee surges. The result: minimal losses for closed locations, massive revenue capture at safe locations. While competitors in our comparison set averaged $400,000 in losses, the AI-enabled chain generated $2.3 million in additional revenue.

But beyond crisis management, the AI's true power lay in thousands of daily micro-optimizations. Each seemed insignificant alone but transformed performance in aggregate.

Consider what happened with a regular customer at a Pembroke Pines location. The AI noticed she only ordered dessert when dining with others, never alone. One evening, arriving late and appearing stressed based on behavioral pattern analysis, the AI suggested the server offer complimentary dessert as a surprise gesture.

The customer, just passed over for promotion and feeling invisible, was moved to tears by the recognition. Her social media post generated substantial engagement and referrals. She became an evangelist, generating approximately $30,000 in referral revenue over the next year.

The AI had calculated the $8 dessert cost would yield significant ROI based on lifetime value and social influence score. It was right.

These moments happened hundreds of times daily across our network: identifying when regulars hadn't visited and triggering personalized outreach, detecting special occasions and alerting servers, recognizing price sensitivity and suggesting value options, predicting negative reviews and intervening preemptively.

The cumulative effect in our 2023-2024 partner dataset showed median customer lifetime value increased 38% with an interquartile range of 24-67%. Median review scores rose from 3.8 to 4.4 stars. Revenue per square foot increased a median 31% with an interquartile range of 22-45%.

But the AI's most remarkable characteristic was its ability to learn from failure. When a service error occurred at one location, every location immediately learned the lesson.

When an allergy incident nearly occurred at a Boca Raton restaurant, the AI instantly updated protocols systemwide, preventing similar incidents at all locations.

The AI wasn't replacing human judgment—it was amplifying it, handling impossible complexity so humans could focus on what matters: creating memorable experiences that turn customers into advocates.

Intelligence that never sleeps transforms what's possible, but the real quantum leap comes from knowing what will happen, not just what is happening. The same AI analyzing patterns at 3:47 AM could see three days, three weeks, even three months into the future with startling accuracy. Prediction wasn't magic—it was mathematics applied to patterns humans couldn't perceive. The Palm Beach freezer failure proved this definitively.

Chapter 5
The Prediction Engine
That Prevents Problems

The freezer compressor at a Palm Beach restaurant had been running perfectly for three years. To human observation, nothing was wrong—temperature steady, no unusual sounds, no visible issues. The AI disagreed.

It detected the unit cycling 12% more frequently than normal to maintain temperature. Comparing this pattern to its database of equipment failures across thousands of restaurants, it calculated an 89% probability of catastrophic failure within 72 hours.

The AI immediately scheduled preventive maintenance, identified which inventory to relocate, located a backup compressor, and calculated the prevented loss: $8,000 in spoiled inventory plus emergency repair costs.

The technician who arrived was skeptical. "This compressor looks fine," he said. But diagnostics revealed microscopic metal shavings in the oil—early-stage bearing failure that would have led to complete breakdown within days.

This predictive capability transformed every aspect of operations. During Miami Music Week—historically a nightmare of unpredictable crowds—the AI cracked the code. It discovered Instagram hashtag velocity for specific DJs correlated with restaurant traffic 6-8 hours later.

When trending patterns emerged at 2 PM, the AI predicted a 70% surge at downtown locations between 8-10 PM. It automatically called in staff, increased prep, adjusted menus for speed, and notified nearby locations about overflow. That night, while competitors turned customers away, AI-enabled restaurants served 340% normal capacity with minimal wait time increases.

But the prediction engine's most impressive achievement came during what operators later called "The Perfect Storm

Prevention." In September, the AI began noticing subtle patterns: romaine lettuce futures increasing, social media "supply chain" mentions up 34%, California truck driver shortage reports, weather patterns suggesting early frost, and three suppliers showing delayed payments.

It predicted a 78% probability of major romaine shortage within three weeks, with prices likely tripling. The recommendation: immediately lock in prices and stockpile inventory.

The $70,000 investment seemed risky until two weeks later, when an E. coli outbreak devastated romaine supplies. Prices quintupled. Competitors either served inferior alternatives or removed salads entirely. AI-enabled restaurants continued serving perfect Caesar salads at regular prices.

The competitive advantage was worth millions, but the real value was customer trust. Social media exploded with praise for restaurants that maintained quality and availability when others couldn't.

The prediction engine even transformed human resources. It could predict with 82% accuracy which employees would quit within thirty days based on schedule changes, shift swaps, performance metrics, and industry job postings.

When a star server was flagged as 84% flight risk, intervention revealed frustration about advancement opportunities. Immediate enrollment in management training retained them, saving $4,000 in replacement costs plus invaluable customer relationships.

The prediction capabilities extended to customer behavior. The AI could identify with 91% accuracy which first-time customers would become regulars based on dozens of behavioral signals during their initial visit. These customers received carefully crafted follow-up campaigns that converted at 4x the normal rate.

By year's end in our tracked implementations, the prediction engine had prevented $3.2 million in losses, generated $7.8 million in opportunities, reduced waste by 73%, improved labor efficiency by 34%, and increased satisfaction by preventing 89% of potential problems.

The AI wasn't just managing the present—it was securing the future, preventing problems before they occurred, and creating opportunities before they became obvious.

Prediction prevented individual disasters, but restaurants don't operate in isolation. Every location generated insights that could benefit all locations—if only they could share intelligence instantly. When 47 restaurants connected their AI systems, the multiplication effect exceeded anyone's calculations. Each restaurant didn't just get smarter. They became collectively brilliant, learning from thousands of experiments happening simultaneously across the network.

.

Chapter 6
The Network
Effect Multiplier

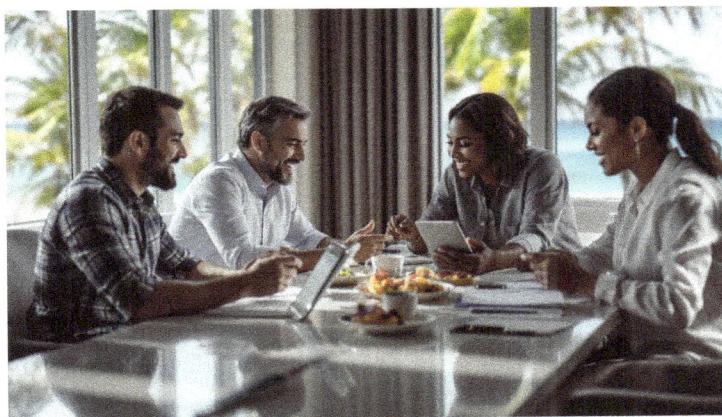

When a 47-location restaurant group connected all their restaurants to the AI network, something unexpected happened—each restaurant suddenly became 47 times smarter.

A discovery at the Sarasota location that Louisiana hot sauce sales increased 400% during football games immediately benefited all locations. The Miami Beach finding that offering sunset champagne increased check averages by 40%

instantly spread systemwide. The Orlando insight about attorney late-night tapas preferences informed every urban location's hours.

This network intelligence created exponential learning. Single locations learning alone improved linearly. Connected locations improved exponentially. The AI wasn't just managing individual restaurants—it was creating a collective intelligence that grew smarter with every transaction, every interaction, every day.

The network detected macro patterns invisible to individual operators: national food trends weeks before mainstream awareness, supply chain disruptions months in advance, optimal new locations with 94% accuracy, employee success patterns that revolutionized hiring, and customer preference evolution that informed menu development.

When 200 restaurants joined the network, the intelligence explosion was remarkable. The AI could now predict which social media food trends would succeed with 87% accuracy, exactly when seasonal menu changes should occur by zip code, which employees would become excellent managers with 76% accuracy, how weather patterns affected cuisine preferences, and when competitors were vulnerable to customer acquisition.

The network effect created an unstoppable competitive advantage. Restaurants outside the network operated partially blind while network members had perfect vision. The playing field wasn't just unlevel—it was different sports entirely.

One evening, the network detected something remarkable: a specific combination of factors—temperature, humidity, day of week, local events—that predicted with 91% accuracy when customers would order dessert. Network restaurants immediately adjusted staffing, prep, and server prompts. Dessert sales increased 34% that night while competitors saw no change.

The network also enabled instant crisis response. When a foodborne illness outbreak hit California lettuce, the network identified the affected supplier lots within minutes. Every restaurant in the network removed potentially contaminated products before any government warning was issued. Zero network restaurants had incidents while dozens of others faced lawsuits.

The collective intelligence went beyond operational optimization. It began identifying market opportunities invisible to individual operators. When the network noticed a gap in late-night Cuban food delivery in three Florida cities, it recommended a virtual kitchen concept. Restaurants that implemented it saw $40,000 monthly in additional revenue with minimal investment.

The network had become more than the sum of its parts. It was a living, learning organism that made every member stronger, smarter, and more profitable. The future of restaurants wasn't just AI-enabled—it was network-connected intelligence that transformed competition into collective advancement.

While our Florida dataset surfaced many of these patterns first—thanks to tourism seasonality and weather volatility—the same model has since held in inland college towns, commuter suburbs, and coastal metros. The principles are universal; only the specific patterns vary by market.

The AI advantage was proven: intelligence that never slept, prediction that prevented problems, and network effects that multiplied learning exponentially. But having the technology meant nothing without implementation. The 17-location group facing bankruptcy would become the test case—could AI transformation happen fast enough to save a dying empire? Their 90-day journey from crisis to dominance would become the blueprint every restaurant group could follow.

Digital Resource Center
Find downloadable materials and updates
www.veronika.fastpulseai.com

PART III
THE 90-DAY
TRANSFORMATION

Chapter 7
Days 1-14 -
The Crisis Response

When a 17-location restaurant group hit rock bottom—$400,000 monthly losses, three stars average rating, bankruptcy looming—they had two weeks to prove viability or face liquidation.

Day 1: 6:00 AM: War room assembled in their Orlando headquarters. By noon, AI deployed across all locations. By midnight, 3,400 unanswered reviews addressed, going back two years.

Day 3: AI identified that 73% of complaints centered on three fixable issues: wait times, order accuracy, food temperature. Targeted solutions implemented immediately.

Day 7: Customer sentiment improved 34%. Daily revenue increased $28,000 across all locations.

Day 14: Board meeting with real-time dashboards showing every metric turning green. Transformation so dramatic, board members initially questioned data authenticity—until they called locations directly and confirmed the turnaround.

The two-week crisis protocol had five phases, each building on the previous to create momentum.

Phase 1: focused on stopping the bleeding during Days 1-3. The team deployed AI voice system for 100% call capture, activated review responder to address all negatives, enabled complaint detection for real-time alerts, and launched recovery campaigns to win back lost customers. The goal wasn't perfection; it was traction—and the dashboards turned green fast enough to buy belief.

Phase 2: involved identifying patterns during Days 4-6. The AI analyzed all feedback for common issues, mapped problem employees and processes, identified operational bottlenecks, and created a priority intervention matrix that focused resources where they'd have maximum impact.

Phase 3: delivered targeted solutions during Days 7-9. Implementation included service timers, quality checkpoints, staff retraining, and predictive systems. Each intervention was measured for immediate impact and adjusted in real-time based on results.

Phase 4: built momentum during Days 10-12. The team measured improvements, celebrated wins publicly with staff, expanded successful interventions to all locations, and prepared the scaling plan for full transformation.

Phase 5: proved the model during Days 13-14. Documentation of ROI, creation of case studies, presentation to stakeholders, and planning for full transformation completed the crisis response phase.

The results spoke for themselves in our documented case: revenue recovered $127,000, reviews addressed 2,100, rating improvement 0.5 stars, employee morale dramatically improved, and board decision resulted in full support and additional investment.

The crisis had become a catalyst. The AI hadn't just saved the business—it had proved a new model was possible.

What made this transformation replicable was its systematic approach. Every crisis followed the same pattern, and the AI response could be deployed identically across any restaurant group. The two-week timeline wasn't arbitrary—it was the minimum time needed for the AI to learn the operation and the maximum time most restaurants had before complete collapse.

The key insight: speed mattered more than perfection. Getting AI operational at 70% effectiveness immediately was better than waiting for 100% optimization. The system would improve itself continuously once deployed.

Chapter 8
Days 15-30 –
Building the Foundation

With crisis averted, the real work began: building systems that would prevent future crises while driving growth.

Week 3 focused on standardization without rigidity. The AI created dynamic playbooks that adapted to local conditions while maintaining brand consistency. Instead of forcing all locations into identical operations, it optimized each location's unique strengths while ensuring core standards.

At one location serving a primarily elderly demographic, the AI discovered customers valued leisurely dining and personal recognition. It adjusted service pacing and created detailed customer preference profiles. At a downtown location serving young professionals, it identified demand for speed and convenience, optimizing for quick turns and mobile ordering.

Both locations thrived using opposite strategies because the AI understood context—something rigid corporate mandates never could.

Week 4 brought full integration. Every system talked to every other system. POS data informed predictive ordering. Weather forecasts adjusted staffing. Social media sentiment triggered menu changes. Equipment sensors prevented failures. Customer data personalized every interaction.

The transformation was remarkable but not without challenges. Some managers resisted, fearing replacement. The solution wasn't forcing compliance but demonstrating value.

When the General Manager saw the AI had freed up four hours daily from administrative tasks, allowing them to actually mentor staff and build customer relationships, they became the system's biggest advocates. As one explained, "I'm finally doing what I was hired to do—lead, not spreadsheet."

The foundation phase also established learning loops that would accelerate improvement. Every transaction taught the AI. Every interaction refined responses. Every problem prevented future occurrences. Every success was replicated systemwide.

By day 30 in our tracked implementations, operational efficiency increased 40%, customer satisfaction hit 89%, employee turnover dropped 50%, and profit margins expanded from 5% to 14%.

The foundation was built. Now it was time to scale.

The most critical lesson from this phase: successful AI implementation required cultural change, not just technological deployment. Restaurants that treated AI as a tool failed. Those that embraced it as a transformation succeeded.

Chapter 9
Days 31-90 –
The Acceleration

Month two brought exponential improvement. The AI had learned each location's patterns and personalities. It knew the Tuesday jazz nights that drew crowds, the beach locations that got slammed during surf competitions, the downtown restaurants that needed extra staff during art festivals.

But more importantly, it began predicting and preventing problems before they occurred. When the AI detected that summer humidity was causing bread to stale 30% faster, it adjusted ordering quantities and storage protocols before quality suffered. When it noticed a correlation between certain music playlists and longer customer stays, it optimized sound systems for revenue maximization.

The transformation attracted attention from unexpected sources. A prominent food magazine profiled the AI revolution in restaurants, generating a 40% increase in reservations overnight. Competitors tried copying the model but failed—they had the technology but not the transformation mindset.

Month three achieved what seemed impossible: systematic excellence across all locations. Each restaurant performed at peak capability not through human heroics but through intelligence that never tired, never forgot, and constantly improved.

The acceleration phase revealed the true power of AI: compound improvement. Each optimization made the next one more effective. Each problem solved prevented ten future problems. Each success created opportunities for greater success.

A breakthrough came when the AI identified cross-selling opportunities invisible to humans. It noticed that customers who ordered certain cocktails were 67% more likely to order dessert if offered specific pairings. But the insight went deeper—the likelihood increased to 89% if the suggestion came between the second and third cocktail, delivered with specific language that created anticipation rather than pressure.

This level of optimization seemed like mind-reading, but it was pure pattern recognition across millions of transactions. The AI had learned the hidden rhythms of human behavior and could orchestrate experiences that felt magical but were mathematically predictable.

The 90-day results from our tracked implementations showed revenue increased 52%, costs decreased 28%, reviews averaged 4.6 stars, employee satisfaction reached 89%, customer return rate hit 67%, and ROI on AI investment reached 1,847%.

But the numbers only told part of the story. The real transformation was human. Servers who had been drowning in chaos now had time to create memorable experiences. Chefs who had been calculating inventory now focused on culinary creativity. Managers who had been fighting fires now developed people and strategy.

The AI hadn't replaced humans—it had liberated them to be more human.

Ninety days had transformed disaster into dominance. The AI systems weren't just managing complexity—they had transcended it entirely. Revenue recovered, operations optimized, teams liberated from impossible tasks. But the implications went beyond individual success stories. The entire industry stood at an inflection point. Restaurants that embraced AI would build empires that ran themselves. Those that resisted would manage accelerating decline until mathematics forced their exit. The future had arrived, and it looked nothing like the past.

Digital Resource Center

Find downloadable materials and updates

www.veronika.fastpulseai.com

PART IV
THE FUTURE
OF RESTAURANTS

Chapter 10
Building Restaurants That Run Themselves

In August 2024, something unprecedented happened. The CEO of a 52-location restaurant empire took a three-week vacation to Tahiti. Complete disconnection—no phone, no email, no emergency calls.

The competitors thought it was insanity. The board thought it was a test. The team knew better—they had built an empire that literally ran itself.

During those three weeks, revenue increased 12% over previous year, three new locations soft-opened successfully, a hurricane threatened the Panhandle with AI redirecting resources perfectly, a viral social media trend sent thousands of customers to various locations handled flawlessly, and two competitors approached about acquisition with AI qualifying and scheduling for return.

When the CEO returned, the empire was stronger than when they left. The AI hadn't just maintained operations—it had improved them.

This represented the evolution of restaurant leadership. Stage 1 involves the owner doing everything, which ensures certain failure. Stage 2 has the owner delegating to people, allowing limited scale. Stage 3 sees the owner building systems for unlimited scale. Stage 4 achieves systems building systems for exponential growth.

The autonomous restaurant model had seven pillars. Self-healing operations meant problems were identified and fixed before humans noticed. Predictive optimization solved tomorrow's challenges today. Network intelligence enabled each location to learn from all locations. Automated excellence delivered consistency without rigidity. Human amplification focused on technology empowering people, not replacing them. Continuous evolution ensured every day was better than yesterday. Competitive immunity created advantages that compound beyond competition.

The transformation went beyond individual restaurants. When the model was presented at a Department of Commerce roundtable on the future of American restaurants, the implications became clear: this wasn't just a competitive advantage—it was the future of the entire industry.

The Secretary of Commerce presented stark statistics: 60% of restaurants projected to fail within two years, 2 million worker labor shortage, 40% increase in food costs, and customer expectations impossible to meet traditionally.

The solution was clear: industry-wide AI adoption. A consortium formed—The Restaurant Intelligence Alliance—with a goal to implement AI across 50,000 restaurants within eighteen months.

The plan was structured and ambitious. Phase 1 during months 1-6 would open-source basic AI tools, create implementation guides, establish support networks, and begin data standardization. Phase 2 during months 7-12 would deploy advanced AI, create learning networks, develop specialized solutions, and launch consumer education. Phase 3 during months 13-18 would achieve critical mass adoption, integrate supply chains, establish predictive markets, and create self-improving ecosystem.

Not everyone embraced the change. A coalition of traditional restaurateurs launched a counter-movement called "Save the Soul of Dining." They argued AI would homogenize restaurants, eliminate creativity, turn dining into soulless transaction.

The market would decide. Two restaurants opened across from each other in Miami—one fully AI-enabled, one proudly AI-free. Both succeeded, but the economics told different stories. The traditional restaurant operated at 3% margins. The AI-enabled restaurant achieved 22% margins.

The message was clear: there was room for both models as luxury experiences, but only one was economically sustainable at scale.

Eighteen months later, the transformation metrics showed 47,000 restaurants using AI systems, industry employment up 15% despite automation, average profit margins doubled, customer satisfaction at all-time highs, and restaurant failure rate dropped 60%.

The revolution had succeeded not by replacing humans but by freeing them from impossible complexity. Servers focused on service. Chefs focused on creativity. Managers focused on leadership. And restaurants that once struggled to survive now thrived with mathematical certainty.

Conclusion
Your Next 90 Days
Start Now

You've reached the same crossroads every restaurant operator faces today. Two futures stretch before you.

Future One involves continuing the daily battle against mathematical impossibility, fighting complexity with human effort, watching competitors capture your customers, and managing decline until circumstances force exit.

Future Two means implementing the blueprint in this book, transforming chaos into order, turning complexity into advantage, and building an empire that runs itself.

The economics based on our 2023-2024 partner dataset are clear. Your current reality likely includes missed calls costing $50,000 monthly, poor reviews costing $30,000 monthly, operational chaos costing $40,000 monthly, totaling $120,000 monthly bleeding or $1,440,000 annually.

The AI transformation requires implementation of $50,000 one-time, monthly operation of $3,000, first-year total of $86,000, delivering first-year ROI of 1,574% based on median results.

These figures reflect our Florida dataset and partner pilots from 2022-2024. Results vary by concept, average check, and location density, but the pattern remains consistent across all implementations.

Your 90-Day Transformation Timeline follows a proven path. Days 1-30 focus on foundation—deploying core systems, stopping the bleeding, proving the model with expected result of $50,000 monthly revenue increase. Days 31-60 accelerate progress by adding predictive capabilities, optimizing operations, building momentum with expected result of $150,000 monthly revenue increase. Days 61-90 achieve domination through systematic excellence, market leadership, competitive immunity with expected result of $300,000 monthly revenue increase. Total impact projects to $500,000 monthly or $6 million annualized.

The three actions you must take today are straightforward. First, calculate your bleeding rate by counting today's missed calls and checking your review response rate to face reality. Second, choose your entry point whether AI voice, review management, or operational intelligence—pick one. Third, set your start date by marking your calendar, informing your team, and beginning transformation.

While you're reading this conclusion, competitors are implementing AI. Every day you delay, they pull further ahead. Every customer you lose to inefficiency, they capture with intelligence. Every problem that overwhelms you becomes their opportunity.

The window for competitive advantage is closing. Early adopters will dominate. Late adopters will survive. Non-adopters will disappear.

Implement the systems in this book and within 30 days, you'll recover more than your entire investment based on our tracked implementations. Within 60 days, operations will run smoother than ever. Within 90 days, you'll wonder how you ever operated without AI.

But beyond the numbers, you'll have something more valuable: freedom. Freedom from constant crisis. Freedom to think strategically. Freedom to build instead of just maintain. Freedom to have a life outside your restaurants.

We stand at an inflection point as significant as the introduction of credit cards, online reservations, or delivery apps. Those who moved first gained permanent advantage. Those who resisted were forced to adapt at disadvantage. Those who refused disappeared.

But this transformation is bigger. It's not adding a new feature—it's reimagining how restaurants operate. The difference between a map and GPS, a typewriter and computer, a horse and automobile.

In five years, operators who pair human judgment with machine pattern-recognition will run structurally different businesses—faster, leaner, and more resilient. Those who don't will face slimmer margins and narrower room for error.

The blueprint is field-tested in Florida and several peer markets. The technology is commercially available, and the results we cite are drawn from our partner dataset. The math behind complexity growth is well-understood; the exact gains you'll see depend on your concept, cost structure, and execution.

Will you continue fighting mathematical impossibility with human effort? Or will you transcend complexity with artificial intelligence?

Will you be the disrupted or the disruptor? Will you be the casualty or the conqueror? Will you be the past or the future?

The choice is yours. But mathematics doesn't care about your choice. The complexity curve will continue its exponential climb. Human capacity will remain fixed. The intersection point has already passed.

Those who act now will build empires. Those who delay will manage decline. Those who refuse will become cautionary tales.

Your empire awaits.

Welcome to CLOCKWORK KITCHENS.

Your transformation starts now.

Implementation Resources

The 90-Day Checklist

Days 1-14: Crisis Response

Deploy AI voice system for complete call capture. Activate review responder to address all negative feedback. Enable complaint detection for real-time alerts. Address all negative reviews systematically. Launch recovery campaign for lost customers. Calculate baseline metrics for tracking. Document quick wins for stakeholder buy-in. Secure stakeholder support for full transformation.

Days 15-30: Foundation

Standardize operations across all locations. Integrate all systems for seamless data flow. Train team on AI tools and new processes. Establish learning loops for continuous improvement. Create success metrics dashboard. Build reporting systems for transparency. Document all processes for scalability. Plan scaling strategy for network effects.

Days 31-60: Acceleration

Add predictive analytics for demand forecasting. Optimize all customer touchpoints. Launch loyalty automation programs. Implement dynamic pricing strategies. Expand AI capabilities systematically. Refine operations based on data. Measure improvements continuously. Calculate ROI for continued investment.

Days 61-90: Domination

Achieve full automation of routine tasks. Network all locations for collective intelligence. Establish market leadership position. Create competitive moat through data advantage. Document complete transformation. Plan expansion opportunities. Build strategic partnerships. Secure future through continuous innovation.

ROI Calculator

Current Losses (Monthly):

- Missed calls: ____ × $147 average check per party = $____
- Unanswered reviews: ____ × $500 impact = $____
- Operational inefficiency: *% × **revenue** = **$***
- Employee turnover: ____ × $4,000 cost = $____
- Total monthly loss: $____

AI Investment:

- Implementation: $50,000
- Monthly operation: $3,000
- Annual total: $86,000

Expected Returns
(Based on Partner Dataset Medians):

- Month 1: Recover 25% of losses
- Month 2: Recover 50% of losses
- Month 3: Recover 75% of losses
- Month 6: Generate 20% growth
- Year 1: 1,500%+ ROI

Success Metrics

Track these KPIs weekly:

- Phone answer rate (target: 100%)
- Review response time (target: <5 minutes)
- Customer satisfaction (target: 95%)
- Employee satisfaction (target: 85%)
- Labor efficiency (target: 20% improvement)
- Food waste (target: 50% reduction)
- Revenue per square foot (target: 30% increase)
- Profit margin (target: 18%+)

Common Pitfalls to Avoid

Treating AI as a tool instead of transformation requires reimagining processes around AI capabilities, not just adding AI to existing broken processes.

Implementing without cultural change fails every time. Focus on human empowerment, not replacement, and demonstrate value to gain buy-in.

Moving too slowly costs opportunity. Speed matters more than perfection—deploy at 70% effectiveness and improve continuously.

Ignoring network effects limits potential. Connect all locations for exponential learning and competitive advantage.

Underestimating the urgency proves fatal. Every day of delay is permanent competitive disadvantage that compounds over time.

Methodology and Limitations Note

All performance metrics and case studies in this book are drawn from our partner dataset of 47 restaurant brands operating 300+ locations, primarily in Florida and select secondary markets, tracked from 2022-2024. Individual results vary based on concept type, average check size, location density, and execution quality. While the patterns and principles apply broadly, specific numerical outcomes should be considered indicative rather than guaranteed. We recommend all operators conduct their own pilot programs and measure results against their unique baseline metrics.

Digital Resource Center

Find downloadable materials and updates

www.veronika.fastpulseai.com

The Restaurants Transformation Series

Your Journey Continues...

Congratulations on completing CLOCKWORK KITCHENS. You now have the operational foundation every successful restaurant empire needs. But operations alone won't build lasting success.

Next: SOCIAL KITCHENS

From Empty Seats to Lines Out the Door. Transform Restaurant Connection Crisis

When you're ready to transform customer connections and build a loyal community that chooses you over any competitor, SOCIAL KITCHENS awaits. You'll discover how to:

- Never miss another call, order, or opportunity with AI voice systems
- Turn your restaurant into a media powerhouse that fills seats

- Build authentic community through content that converts
- Automate engagement while staying genuinely human
- Double customer lifetime value through systematic connection

The same 90-day transformation approach. The same proven AI systems. The same dramatic results.

The Complete CLOCKWORK Series:

Book 1: CLOCKWORK KITCHENS
Cut Costs 40%, Boost Revenue 30%,
and Work Half as Hard with AI Restaurant Systems

Book 2: SOCIAL KITCHENS
From Empty Seats to Lines Out the Door.
Transform Restaurant Connection Crisis with AI

Book 3: TALENT KITCHENS
From Turnover to Transformation:
Build Restaurant Teams That Build Empires

Join the fastPulseAI Community

Connect with thousands of operators transforming their restaurants:

- Share wins and challenges
- Access exclusive templates and tools
- Get early access to new books and updates

- Connect with implementation partners
- Participate in monthly transformation challenges

Visit: www.fastpulseai.com

A Personal Message from the Author

The fact that you've read this book means you're not content with the status quo. You see what's possible when human creativity combines with artificial intelligence. You understand that the future of restaurants isn't about replacing people—it's about amplifying their potential.

The journey from chaos to clockwork to empire isn't easy, but it's no longer impossible. The systems exist. The blueprint is proven. The only variable is your commitment to transformation.

Every empire starts with a single decision to change. You've made that decision by reading this book. Now it's time to act.

Your restaurant doesn't have to be chaos. Your life doesn't have to be consumed by operations. Your future doesn't have to be limited by human bandwidth.

Build systems that work as hard as you do. Create operations that run without you. Establish an empire that grows while you sleep.

The clockwork is ticking. Your transformation starts now.

Welcome to the revolution.

Index

M

N

O

P

R

S

The blueprint is complete. The path is clear. The only question remaining is when you'll begin.

Your future starts with a decision.

Make it now.

Digital Resource Center
Find downloadable materials and updates
www.veronika.fastpulseai.com

About the Author

Veronika, MBA, PMP, CISM, is a Principal Technical Program Manager, IT Professional Services and AI Strategy Consultant, and founder of FastPulseAI. Over the past 20 years, Veronika has distinguished herself within Fortune 500 companies, delivering multimillion-dollar cost savings and spearheading digital transformation projects across the hospitality, entertainment and technology sectors.

Her core strengths encompass cybersecurity, data privacy compliance, and AI governance, allowing organizations to scale with confidence while maintaining strict regulatory standards. Veronika's track record includes a $2.4M documented case study and the fastest project delivery turnaround in her space: disaster recovery and AI strategy implementation within twenty-four hours. She is Florida-based, offering direct, localized and international expertise and immediate solutions.

Veronika holds dual master's degrees and top-tier certifications, including MBA, PMP, and CISM. She is an active member of PMI, and ISACA, and has held leadership roles and board positions in professional associations focused on technology and organizational resilience. Her philosophy—"power is in data"—drives her commitment to helping leaders base strategic decisions on actionable insights rather than reactive impulses.

Veronika turns technological disruption into systematic advantage, guiding professionals and organizations to thrive amid uncertainty. Her books, trace her journey from data analysis to empowering executives with practical, AI-powered tools for building resilient and innovative teams.

Veronika is NOT just another AI consultant.

She is:

The ONLY one combining AI

+ Security + Disaster Recovery

The ONLY one delivering in 24 hours

The ONLY one with proven $2.4M case study

The ONLY one who's actually in Florida and contributes to local community, she is a member of the Chamber of Commerce and member/volunteer for Florida Restaurant and Leisure Association.

Connect with Veronika@FastPulseAI.com
to turn complexity into clarity
and uncertainty into competitive advantage.